Tourist Trails

In and around Nottinghamshire and Derbyshire

Written and produced by Stephen Thirkill

Index

Acknowledgements	Page 3
Author Foreword	Page 4
Newstead Abbey	Page 5
Teversal Trails	Page 19
Clumber Park	Page 25
King's Mill Reservoir	Page 37
Hardwick Hall	Page 45
Southwell Workhouse	Page 57
Chatsworth House	Page 69

© Chad
ISBN

All rights reserved. Publshed by

Acknowledgements

TOURIST attractions across Nottinghamshire and Derbyshire would certainly not be the success they are today without the vast teams of volunteers who give up their time and effort to help their atttaction thrive.

It is their passion, knowledge and sheer determination which helps bring their particular tourist attraction to life and ensures the nation is left with an enduring legacy which we can all be extremely proud of.

Producing this book would certainly not have been possible without this group of talented and extremely interesting guides, who brought colour, excitement and a variety of must-hear stories to each and every one of my visits.

Judy Williams, who effortlessly guided me through the life and times of Bess of Hardwick at historic Hardwick Hall, is a perfect example. Her wealth of knowledge, along with her endless enthusiasm, on her subject was a pleasure to experience.

Likewise John Twelftree, the guide for Southwell Workhouse, proved to be a fountain of knowledge on the Workhouse experiment throughout the Victorian era, which was wonderful to hear.

Trever Pressley was another man to have captivated my interest during my tour of Clumber Park. My visit to this peaceful sanctuary simply flew by thanks to Trevor's interesting insights and it is heart-warming to see Clumber Park go from strength to strength.

King's Mill Reservoir and Teversal Trails also seem set for a very healthy future, with countryside rangers such as Alan Cordin doing an excellent job in helping the attractions thrive.

Alan effortlessly guided me around the trails and reservoir during two memorable visits. His soothing tones and wonderful wildlife knowledge made for two very entertaining audio tours.

Sue Brown and Kay Rotchford have an attraction to be very proud of. And that passion and enthusiasm was very much in abundance as they guided me around the captivating Chatsworth House. With a blend of beauty and history, it is easy to see why film crews view this Derbyshire delight as a must-use location.

Gillian Crawley, who helped kick off our CD series, is certainly a lady who knows her stuff. During my guide around Newstead Abbey, Gillian presented a wonderful case of why the Abbey, and Lord Byron in particular, has become a place of pilgrimage for many.

Every one of these guides is a personal credit to their organisations and deserve much praise from, not just myself, but everyone who has been treated to one of their guides.

On another personal note, I would like to thank Laura Milner for her drive and professionalism, which helped ensure the smooth production of the CD which accompanies this book, Emma Angell, for her hard work in getting the book produced, and to Ashley Booker and Tim Paget for their work in editing the book.

A thankyou must also go to Matthew Pidcock, whose vision and creativity has helped to make the CD bright, appealing and really stand out.

Last but, of course, not least I would like to extend a special thankyou to Chad editor Tracy Powell for her support in turning this fledgling idea into an exciting reality.

It has always been a long-standing dream of mine to become a published author. Without the hard work of each individual guide and the support of the National Trust, Nottingham City Council and my colleagues at the Chad, this dream would not have been realised and, for that, I remain very grateful to you all.

Author Foreword

COMING from Yorkshire I was largely unaware of the quality of tourist attractions and beauty spots which bless the North Nottinghamshire and Derbyshire area. Looking in from a distance, Mansfield, Ashfield and the wider area is often viewed as an area struggling to recover its ecomony and pride following the devastating collapse of the coal-mining industry.

But nothing could be further from the truth and, as I hope this book helps to illustrate, this region has a vibrant tourist industry and a history to be very proud of.

From the lady who staffs the gift shop or cafe, the tour guide who dedicates countless hours to learning their trade, right up to the managers and directors responsible for shaping the future of the local tourist industry - personal pride and quality are all part of the job.

And it was exactly this pride and passion from all concerned that shone through for me during each and every one of my visits.

It was simply wonderful to experience each individual success story first hand with the tale of Southwell Workhouse - a fantastic preservation of Victorian history which survived the abhorrent threat of being turned into apartments - and Teversal Trail's inspiring transformation from former coal industry railway tracks to beauty spot offering particular pleasure.

On a personal note this series provided me with many

Stephen Thirkill

delightful experiences, with exclusive behind-the-scenes access to Lord Byron's bedroom, the awe-inspiring spiral staircase at Hardwick Hall and the amazing collection of artwork gathered at Chatsworth House especially standing out.

Quite simply our area has a thriving must-visit tourist industry, with its stunning nature, history, architecture and serenity all offering something to keep every visitor entertained.

I hope this book and accompanying CD will go some small way to inspiring you all to get out and sample Nottinghamshire and Derbyshire's delights for yourself.

1 Newstead Abbey

Newstead Abbey

EPISODE GUIDE: Gillian Crawley, Newstead Abbey's Site Manager

AN ENGLISHMAN's home is his castle, or so says the well known proverb. If you learn about the castle then you'll learn about the man.

And perhaps such a saying has never rung truer than when you take a look at the iconic 12th Century Newstead Abbey - a mysterious and romantic setting made famous around the globe by its highest-profile owner.

George Gordon, the 6th Lord Byron, has been labelled as one of the greatest romantic poets of his generation - a reputation for magnificence which is also so much in evidence around his former home.

The abbey, nestled just off the A60 in more than 300 acres of picturesque gardens and parkland, began life as a place of holy worship after its creation as an Augustinian priory by Henry II in about 1170.

The Abbey ruins

A mysterious and romantic setting made famous by its highest profile owner

In 1540, Henry VIII granted Newstead to the poet's ancestor, Sir John Byron, who converted the priory into a house and established his family's connection which still thrives to this day.

Sir John Byron and his successors kept much of the monastic structure and layout so that the house still retains its medieval character, with the eye-catching west front of the church still surviving from the late 13th Century.

But it was thanks to its most inspirational owner that the beautiful abbey was firmly transformed into another place of worship - this time for poetry lovers across the world - and given a legacy which the popular attraction still retains to this very day.

And it was this legacy which I was rather eager to find out much more about when I made my first ever visit to the beautiful abbey for a personal tour around the attraction with my guide, Gillian Crawley.

Inspiring surroundings

As the sun beat down fiercely and the soothing lakes, ponds and water cascades of the abbey's splendid gardens shimmered delightfully in the glorious sunshine, it was rather easy to understand just why George Gordon, who became the sixth Lord Byron in 1798, found these surroundings so inspiring.

The pond

The charming landscape, which owes much of its beauty to the nearby River Leen, includes The Eagle Pond, The Fern Garden, The Spanish Garden and The Japanese Garden, offers the ideal place for quiet, serene and relaxing contemplation capable of getting any poet's creative juices flowing freely.

And it was certainly the case for the revered Lord Byron, who became one of the most popular icons of the Romantic Age, with his personal beauty, brilliant mind and reckless spirit

Lord Byron

Like the **superhuman heroes** of his own dark tales, Byron has often been portrayed as mysterious, self-destructive and **proudly defiant**

fascinating his contemporaries and poetry lovers for decades to follow.

Like the superhuman heroes of his own dark tales, Byron has often been portrayed as mysterious, self-destructive and proudly defiant. And, for Gillian, the characteristics of the owner sums up his former castle perfectly.

"The abbey shouldn't still be standing after all this time. Why it hasn't been knocked down after the dissolution of the monastries in 1539 when the abbey was converted into a country house and why it was saved is a mystery," says a rather pleased Gillian.

"But it is certainly for our benefit that it has been saved. The house itself is a great legacy of the fall out from Henry VIII's divorce from Catherine of Aragon and the legacy of Lord Byron and the front of the abbey sets the tone for the whole visit."

"Would Byron still recognise today's surroundings from those where he made his name all those years ago?," I ask Gillian with a touch of curiousity.

"The grounds have not got smaller since Byron's day. There has been a break up of the estate and there are a lot of private properties within the historic bounds, but he would still recognise the modern-day abbey.

"There is gothic romance, there is mystery, there is something unexplained. I think it is a great place to start the visit," gushes Gillian with youthful exuberance and enthusiasm.

And although Byron no longer walks the delightful grounds penning his poetical masterpieces, his inspiration to fellow artists still continues.

"The view is actually very similar to in Byron's day, there is still a lake here, there is still a stable block and the west front and the big bay windows are all still there," said Gillian, whose passion for Lord Byron is evident for all to see.

An artist's paradise

"The grounds of the abbey are an artist's paradise. Lots of amateur artists come down to paint and the visitors love to see them, but Newstead is synonymous with the poet Lord Byron and it is a place of pilgrimage.

"Byron died a great hero and Newstead became a great place of pilgrimage as a result. People want to come and see where the poet lived and we are in a great shrine I suppose."

As Gillian took me inside the historic abbey house, which Lord Byron called home at various times between the autumn of 1808 and autumn 1814, the evidence of Byron's personal touch instantly leapt out with the contents of his library providing a wonderful and everlasting insight into the mind of the genius.

The impressive library, which Gillian clearly took a great delight in showing off, provides some of the great treasures of Newstead Abbey and includes rare annotated books, letters, furniture and manuscripts belonging to the great poet as well as a variety of cherished personal possessions.

"I have two favourites amongst his possessions in this room,"

Boatswain's shrine

Gillian reveals. "One is the collar to his great dog Boatswain, whom Byron built a shrine to following his death from rabies. He was one of the first Newfoundland dogs brought to Britain, and I think the collar must have been one when he was a puppy because those dogs can get very big.

"The other is a tree trunk that, as a young man, he carved his name into.

"What we have in here are some really fascinating portraits." Gillian then points to a magnificent painting above the fireplace of a remarkably modern-looking Lord Byron, which I was suprised to see would not have looked out of place on a Facebook profile.

"Byron very much controlled his image," explains Gillian. "That romantic poet and that image of striving for your art has never gone away and I think maybe Byron invented that."

And it was in this very room that the gifted Byron shot himself to national fame with a series of poems which captured the heart of a public eager to soak up his impressive work.

A remarkable career

Byron embarked on his remarkable career in 1805 and he spent the following three years publishing juvenile poetry, with Fugitive Pieces (printed and withdrawn in November 1806) and Various Occasions (published in January 1807) amongst his early work.

But it was in 1812 that the Cambridge-educated Byron finally enjoyed his big breakthrough, with Childe Harold's Pilgrimage I and II making him instantly famous following its publication on 10th March.

> "He was very much **his own man** and stood up for what he believed in. He did not conform to the establishment."

Two years later the demand for Byron was evident for all to see when The Corsair sold a staggering 10,000 copies on the first day of its publication on 1st February 1814.

Yet there was much more to the charistmatic Byron than just a major gift for penning poetry, with his desire to stand up for the rights of the downtrodden and poor against the establishment making him an instant hero for the general public.

It was just days before the publishing of The Corsair when the honourable Byron showed he was a man clearly ahead of his time when he delivered the first of just three speeches in the House of Lords opposing the death-penalty for industrial sabotage by starving Nottinghamshire workers.

"He was very much his own man who stood up for what he believed in. He did not conform to the establishment which is one of the big appeals of Byron to an awful lot of people," Gillian explains with a great sense of admiration.

"He worked his way up and became someone special," she adds beaming with a warm sense of pride similar to that feeling after a close relation has finally succeeded in his goals.

"One thing that we are very proud of in Nottinghamshire are Byron's speeches to the House of Lords defending the Local

11

Framework Knitters because, for smashing their equipment, they were being punished by deportation and even execution.

"Byron stood up and said that it was wrong and that this crime did not deserve that level of punishment. He had tremendous principles and conscience."

Love and scandal

The poet then stepped back from political life to concentrate on his true love for poetry, producing The Bride of Abydos in 1812, Ode to Napoleon Bounaparte in 1814 as well as Childe Harold III, The Prisoner of Chillon, Darkness, and The Dream

Two years after his exile, Byron finally managed to **offload Newstead Abbey** to the wealthy Thomas Wildman

in 1816 - just a few notable works amongst his many masterpieces.

However, Byron's scandalous love affairs and shockingly disastrous marriage to Annabella in 1815, which ended with her leaving him just one year later, led to very serious financial difficulties and obliged the poet to leave England in 1816.

He then spent the rest of his brief life in exile on the continent while trying to sell off Newstead Abbey to ease his money woes.

It was whilst on the continent that Byron wrote brilliantly upon the quintessentially Romantic themes of personal freedom and political liberty, before he finally died on 19th April 1824 fighting for what he believed in as he tried to help the Greeks win their independence from Turkish rule.

Two years after his exile, Byron finally managed to offload Newstead Abbey to the wealthy Thomas Wildman, who had made his fortune from the family-owned plantations in Jamaica, in 1918 for £94,500.

Wildman then spent this vast wealth repairing and restoring Newstead to its former glory.

Like the Byrons before him, Wildman preserved the medieval style of the house and employed the architect John Shaw to carry out alterations which blended well with the oldest parts of the building.

How thankful the modern day tourists are for Wildman's **attention to detail** and his seemingly bottomless pit of money

Wildman also filled the house with fine old tapestries, ancient armour and antique furniture in keeping with Newstead's long and proud history.

And it was this sale which, according to Gillian, helped repair the ailing fortunes of the abbey and safeguard its future for generations to come.

"He was very instrumental in maintaining the abbey," explains my insightful guide. "When Byron inherited the property, he inherited a property that was very dilapidated and had not been maintained.

"The roof leaked. It was the ancestral home, but a little bit of an eye opener for someone used to more luxurious surroundings.

"Wildman bought the abbey for around £100,000, which was an amazing amount of money for the time.

"He then spent another £100,000 creating the gothic revival home of his dreams and commissioned work of the highest quality."

And how thankful the modern day tourists are for Wildman's attention to detail and his seemingly bottomless pit of money.

In 1861 William Frederick Webb, African explorer and friend of the iconic Dr David Livingstone, purchased the abbey from Thomas Wildman's widow.

After Mr Webb died in 1899, the estate passed to each of his surviving children and finally to his grandson Charles Ian Fraser, who sold Newstead to the Nottinghamshire philanthropist Sir Julien Cahn. He then presented it to Nottingham Corporation in 1931.

And it is thanks to Webb and his exhaustive travelling that Newstead developed another more unknown crown in its jewel.

"This room is my favourite room," reveals Gillian as she draws back the blinds exposing us to the dazzling sunlight and the lush green gardens outside.

Inside the room are walls covered with splendid panels, which I wrongly identify as being African before the knowledgeable Gillian politely puts me right.

"This is called the Japanese room. These panels are tourist souvenirs because the Webb family went to Japan and brought these magnificent panels back.

"There was obviously a fascination with all things Oriental," explains Gillian. "They glitter with gold when you get the sunlight on them, it is lovely to see them in the light."

This particular trend was popular during this period and proved a source of inspiration for artists across Europe.

TIMELINE

1170
Newstead Abbey was originally founded as an Agustinian priory by Henry II in about 1170.

1539
The monastery at Newstead Abbey was dissolved by Henry VIII, putting an end to the small religious community who lived there.

1540
Newstead Abbey becomes the Byron family home when Sir John Byron converted the priory into a house for his family after being granted the estate by Henry VIII.

1798
Lord George Byron, the iconic poet, becomes the sixth Lord Byron on 21st May 1798 following the death of William Byron.

Gillian, who clearly understands her art, adds: "It is about the lives of women in the late Victorian period, about them travelling to Japan, being inspired by Japanese art and bringing back those panels that are of the highest quality, which we see in the room.

"It is the type of art that was inspiring the great French impressionists. They have small panels . . . but we have got a room full of these panels and it is fantastic to see,"'she adds with clear delight.

And who can blame Gillian, for this really is a splendid room which further adds to Newstead's everlasting appeal as a place of mystery, of adventure, of quality, of excitement and artistic appeal.

Lastly, but by no means least, on my captivating adventure around magical Newstead I am taken to the famous medieval cloister, with its peaceful seclusion and beautiful plants the perfect place to gain inspiration.

And, as I stare intently for a moment at the cloister, I can well imagine a certain Lord Byron sat contemplating his next move in life as time ticks slowly by.

"The cloister is one of the last places that you see in the abbey and it is simply wonderful," says Gillian, who rates the cloister as her favourite area to visit on the entire estate.

"The best time to come and see this is either 6am or about 7pm, when you have the place all to yourself. It is quite a magical space."

Our attention then turns to what is perhaps the **strangest sculpture** I have ever seen ...a cross between a bird, a cat and a pig

Our attention then turns to what is perhaps the strangest sculpure I have ever seen. It appears to be a cross between a bird, a cat and a pig. What it is no-one knows, but one thing certain is that it won't be doing a roaring trade at the local garden centre this summer.

But, strange as it might be, for Gillian the unusual and mysterious item sums up Newstead Abbey better than any other item we have seen so far on this flying visit.

"There are very few things I would take home from Newstead Abbey, not that I am allowed to do so of course," she says with a gentle chuckle,"but if I ever could, the one thing I would take is one of the animal sculptures in the cloister area.

"It is a bit of a pig, he's got buttefly wings and a cat face with very long ears and long legs." Gillian scratches her head in a rather bemused fashon.

"I don't know what type of animal he was, but he would have pride of place on my fireplace at home, the sculpture is Newstead for me and all that it is about."

TIMELINE

1818
The estate was bought for £94,500 by Thomas Wildman, a friend from Byron's school days, after Lord Byron fell into financial difficulties.

1861
William Frederick Webb, African explorer and friend of Dr David Livingstone, purchased the abbey from Thomas Wildman's widow.

1899
Webb died in 1899, with the estate passing to each of his surviving children, and finally to his grandson Charles Ian Fraser.

1931
Fraser sold Newstead to Nottinghamshire philanthropist Sir Julien Cahn, who presented it to Nottingham Corporation in 1931.

Interesting facts

■ The 12th Century abbey was originally founded as an Augustinian priory, named the priory of St. Mary of Newstead.

■ Musket balls and bullet holes can still be seen in the front walls of Newstead Abbey from when the building was attacked by Parliamentary forces during the English Civil War.

■ The famous explorer Dr Livingstone spent six months of his life living at Newstead Abbey during the mid 1860s after becoming friends with abbey owner William Frederick Webb during an expedition in Africa.

■ The abbey's original surviving West Front dates back to the 13th Century.

■ The fountain in the abbey's medieval cloister dates back to the 1630s.

■ The annual income of the priory in 1534 was thought to be £167 16s. 11d, which equates to £70,000 a year in current money.

■ Newstead had been the Byron family home since 1540 when Sir John Byron acquired it from Henry VIII.

■ The first Lord Byron was granted his title as a reward for his loyalty to King Charles I during the English Civil War in the 1640s.

■ In 1818 the estate was purchased for £94,500 by Thomas Wildman, a friend from Byron's school days, after Lord Byron fell into financial difficulties.

■ Despite Newstead Abbey being synonymous with Lord Byron, the famous poet lived in the Abbey for just six years.

■ The lake was dredged in the late 18th Century and the lectern, thrown into the abbey fishpond by the monks to save it during the dissolution of the monasteries, was discovered.
  In 1805 it was given to Southwell Minster by Archdeacon Kaye where it still resides.

Facilities
■ Cafe with outdoor dining
■ Guided tours
■ Educational visits
■ Extensive gardens
■ Disabled toilets
■ Gift shop

T 01623 455 900 **E** newstead.abbey@nottinghamcity.gov.uk **W** www.newsteadabbey.org.uk

2 Teversal Trails

Teversal Trails

■ **EPISODE GUIDE:** Alan Cordin, countryside ranger at Ashfield District Council

THE MENTAL scars left by the collapse of the coal industry across Nottinghamshire and Derbyshire may still be there, but the physical reminders have all but disappeared in one area of the two counties.

Left with a seriously dented pride and reputation, thousands of jobs forever consigned to history and a shattered economy, the area could either accept its fate or fight back. To start again and create a new industry capable of rebuilding the local economy and getting people back into work.

And in Teversal, as with many other areas across the region, the determined locals have bravely fought back with one group of nature lovers and conservationists, along with Ashfield District Council, joining forces to transform the area's disused pit railway tracks into a new recreation area as part of the wider plan to regenerate the deprived district.

Varied walks

The fruits of their labour resulted in the impressive Teversal Trails, a network of 12 varied walks - ranging from one mile to 12 miles - which meander along the track beds of the former colliery railways that served the Mansfield and Ashfield area.

Looking at the setting now it is hard to imagine that this charming woodland retreat, which now resonates to the vibrant chirps and tweets of the many bird species at home here, was once the daily site for hundreds of noisy trains which caused such a blight on Teversal's picturesque and peaceful environment.

Being something of a walking lover myself I was eager to discover the delights of the Trails and the impact this ambitious project has had on the area.

So, with the gentle sunshine providing a lovely warming start to the day, I set out on an exploratory stroll with countryside ranger Alan Cordin, a man charged with maintaining

the Trails for Ashfield District Council, from Teversal Trails Visitor Centre along the old Midland Line to Pleasley Pit Country Park.

"This was the original line that was created to access the pit at Silverhill," explains Alan, a softly-spoken middle-aged man with a real passion for the environment. "It came to Silverhill around 1886 so it's been here for quite a few years."

Even though it is shortly after 10am on a Wednesday morning the trail is already displaying a healthy sprinkling of walkers and bikers eager to soak up some sunshine and fresh air.

"This is a very popular part of the trail since we got the upgrades to create a wider path for people to walk and cycle in safety," Alan says in a happy tone, which reveals a hidden sense of joyous pride. "It is very well used, we have now got more people using the trails than we ever thought we would have.

"Hopefully we can add to this success and we are currently working on some extensions."

Alan's point is perfectly timed as our ears pick up the distant buzzing hum of a JCB and tractor from a group of nearby workmen busily levelling the woodland surface on what is known as the Link Track - a mineral line which linked up the nearby Midland Railway with the Great Northern line in Skegby and Teversal.

And thanks to the determined efforts of the local conservationists, Teversal Trails has now become not just a success story for humans, but also for a variety of rare wildlife which frequent the lush and blooming woods. This includes the rare Dinge Skipper butterfly, which loves bare ground where it can sit and warm up.

"The Trails has a really rich and vibrant eco-system," Alan says in a mood as cheery as the weather around us. "Most of the railways, even today, have good eco-systems with plants, floura and fauna often found by the side of the tracks so this area is no different.

"The tracks are really like motorways for animal and plants," adds Alan with his unique way of assessing the area.
Alan - a graduate of a Countryside Management course at Southwell's Brackenhurst College - became a countryside ranger following a career change and has been walking the captivating Trails for a number of years.

"I got into this thanks to a mid-life crisis," he jokes warmly. "I have always been interested in nature so I decided to do something about it. I had a complete career change and here I am today."

Midlife crisis or not, Alan's sudden change of heart away from the office to the great outdoors has clearly been a blessing in disguise for the good people of Ashfield.

But despite the thousands of pounds being poured into this visionary project, Teversal Trails can only be the success story it is today if nature decides to play ball.

"Nature makes it a real vast success and it helps the quality of life for local people," Alan explains with the excited tone of a child who has just received their perfect Christmas present.

Once he's in full stride there is no stopping him as his true passion for, and belief in, the splendid project begins to shine through as brightly as the sunshine above us.

"People can come just a short distance and within a short time they have moved from Sutton-In-Ashfield, for example, right into the heart of this glorious countryside.

"At the start and end of the summer, the paths are full of vibrant colours and are beautiful to walk along. Winter is also nice with the freshness in the air providing a nice walk and the snow making the fields look rather lovely.

"Really the Trails are ever changing and fluctuating with the weather and the seasons. There is something for everyone here."

And it is not just humans who are flocking to the Trails as Alan, who appears to have every trail firmly printed onto his brain like a map, is quick to point out.

Fantastic birdlife

"Teversal is a great place to be with lots of history, scenery and lots of fantastic birds. At the last bird count we had 87 different species over the year."

"That's a really big number," I blurt out as I struggle to hide my surprise.

"We get a lot of migrant birds so that total includes our summer and winter visitors," says Alan with a flourish as he puts the impressive total into some sort of context.

"We have a very diverse habitat," he adds with a broad youthful grin. "There are probably more species if we add on to what they get at Pleasley, there will be some that only drop off because the Pleasley end of the Trails is on a migration route.

"They will come in and feed up before going on their way. They may only visit twice a year but they all count."

I can think of better places to go for my holiday than Pleasley, but it certainly seems to do the job for our feathered friends.

As we make our way down the line the pathway is slowly transformed from an expansive open setting under a punishing sun into a beautiful green woodland vista complete with a roof

A monument to the trail's former mining heritage

An old bridge

of overhanging trees blocking out the climbing sun - no doubt providing refreshing shade for any walkers taking on the trail during the height of summer.

The narrow pathway is now only just big enough for Alan and myself to walk alongside as the thick untamed bushes and brambles continue their seemingly unstoppable summer growth all along the steep sided former railway embankments. To our right we leave Teversal village and its rich history, which includes the Grade I listed St Catherine's Church dating back to the Norman period, behind us as we push on to our goal.

Further down the trail many imposing ash trees soar high into the sky along the side of the path creating a Sherwood Forest-style vista - yet another illustration of the many changing faces of this delightful trail.

But, although the similarities with the most famous Nottinghamshire woodland in the world is there for all to see, Alan is eager to point out the unique individuality of this compelling countryside.

"Maintaining such a varied trail poses us with many difficult challenges."

"We have changed from a meadow down the road to a woodland, so it is yet another change in habitat. As we continue down the trail it will begin to open up again into a meadow. Maintaining such a varied trail poses us with many different challenges. We are constantly cutting back the scrub and felling some of the bigger trees if necessary."

"So do you see yourself in competition with Sherwood Forest?," I ask a touch mischeviously.

"No not at all," Alan says without doubt. "This is a different habitat which offers a different way of walking for people.

"Sherwood Forest is ancient woodland, they have heathland, we don't. Really it is totally different here for walkers."

A common theme which I have picked up on during my various travels across the district is the strong desire to unite together to help further

develop an expansive Nottinghamshire tourist industry and regenerate local pride. Teversal Trails, as Alan eagerly confirms, is no different. "Having Sherwood Forest and Clumber Park so close on our doorstep is not a threat to us, it is good for tourism in this area," he says as he passionately explains the bigger picture to me.

"We have lost the coal industry, we have lost the knitting and garments industry, so we have got to encourage and develop a new industry for Mansfield and Ashfield and I think tourism is essential to this.

"It is also good for local pride and people are much happier to say they are from Teversal as a result."

We then cross the border into Derbyshire - giving me some child-like delight in the knowledge that I have walked across two counties - as our end target of Pleasley Pit slowly closes in.

As we pass Lady Spencer's Wood on our left, the light breeze slowly begins to develop into a pushy and increasingly strong headwind. To our right way out on the horizon the cranes working to develop Sutton's King's Mill Hospital become visible, as is a rather beautiful field full of bright red poppies. It's a stunning cheery view, which certainly helps to encapsulate all that is so good and positive about Teversal Trails.

Finally, we see the welcoming site of Pleasley Pit Country Park, which offers some splendid and commanding views of miles and miles of the surrounding countryside, as well as the old chimney and winding gear used to such good effect when the pit was the lifeblood of the village.

Alan pauses for a moment. "If you listen you can hear a train in the background and the song of the skylark. From industrial heritage to the natural world, what a fantastic site it is," he beams.

It certainly is a wonderfully nostalgic way to bring an end to our gentle stroll which has taken me, not just down three miles of countryside paths, but also down decades of proud industrial heritage and the memories of the families living in the houses we now see littering the horizon.

The pits and the colliery tracks are gone forever, but it is clear that they will forever remain an unforgettable part of the life and soul of this proud area. Gone but not forgotten.

Facilities
- Free parking
- Wheelchair access to visitor centre, toilets and trail access
- Refreshments, hot snacks available
- Suitable for school parties
- Souvenirs
- Ideal for nature studies

Info: 01623 442021   W www.teversaltrails.com

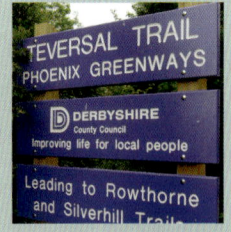

3 Clumber Park

Clumber Park

EPISODE GUIDE: Trevor Pressley, visitor services manager

SEVENTY years ago picturesque Clumber Park hid a dark military secret as it played its part in helping the nation defeat the even darker forces of Nazi Germany.

Between 1939 and 1945 the green and idyllic beauty spot roared to the noise of the military rather than tourists following its requisition by the Army for use as a war-time ammunition dump.

Nowadays a young visitor exploring the estate's vast double-sided Lime Tree Avenue, which at three miles long and with 1296 trees is Europe's longest avenue of lime trees, may come across a squirrel or some wildlife going about its business.

But, in 1940, they would have discovered a huge arsenal of 60,000 tonnes of ammunition capable of wiping out centuries of Clumber's history in a flash.

As well as being home to an army of high explosives Clumber Park, or ammunition sub depot 24 as it was then known, was also used for secret trials of a 77ft long trench-digging tank code-named Nellie, which was capable of moving a staggering 100 tonnes of earth per minute.

The project was the brainchild of war Prime Minister Winston Churchill, who became Clumber Park's most famous visitor when he travelled to this part of North Nottinghamshire, under the alias of Colonel Warden, in November 1941 to inspect the scheme's progress.

And it is a visit that still proudly lives on in folklore for all those connected with Clumber Park, according to Trevor Pressley, the attraction's bubbly and instantly likeable visitor services manager who was to be my guide for the day.

"At any one time during this period Clumber had 60,000 tonnes of ordnance stored," Trevor explains in his umistakable, calm manner. "The huge expansive grassland on the south side of the lake was used for this secret project.

The Lime Tree Avenue

The Walled Garden

Clumber Park was also used for secret trials of a 77ft long trench-digging tank code-named Nellie

The property, which became the family seat for the 2nd Duke of Newcastle in 1768, was purchased by The National Trust for £75,000 - £45,000 of which was raised by the public.

The Army finally vacated Clumber in 1955, allowing the land to return to public use, and it has not looked back since.

And, just like Britain during the early stages of The Second World War, Clumber is also very adept at self-sufficiency and standing on its own two feet.

Walled Garden

The attraction's delightful and well-restored Walled Garden plays a key part in this philosophy, as the knowledgeable Trevor is more than happy to explain.

"This is a spectacular place in the summer which goes down very well with the visitors. This year we have had record numbers

"Nellie was made in Lincoln and brought to Clumber in 27 different pieces under cover of darkness.

"Churchill had been Minister for Defence during The First World War and was convinced that the latest war would be another trench war, so he designed this machine. It is a proud part of Clumber's history," Trevor concludes.

But from those dark days of war, tension, pain and suffering, Clumber Park rapidly evolved into one of the county's premier leisure and recreation environments as well as a haven for a vast variety of trees, rare plants and wildlife.

"That is the wonderful thing about this property, it is **magnificent** all year round."

into the garden itself, and we are looking to top 40,000 visitors," he adds with high expectation.

"This garden, during the time of the Duke of Newcastle, would have provided food for the house and his guests but now it provides fruit and veg produce for our cafe and restaurant. There's a lot of creativity behind this garden."

Local is very much a buzzword around these parts with Clumber doing all it can to boost the area's economy by supporting local tradesmen.

"We try wherever possible to stock local products," Trevor passionately adds as he does his bit to promote a reduction in food miles. "That ties in with what we do with our local food message of using locally sourced meat, dairy products and organic and seasonal products wherever possible.

"We have to support our local economy, the people who come here and our environment. It brings a lot of benefits for us all."

The Gardens

The Grounds

Woodland Walks

As we make our way out of the Walled Garden Trevor, whose role it is to promote all that is excellent about Clumber, begins to get into full swing.

"There are lots of lovely woodland walks around the property for people to come and experience," he says as he battles through the crisp autumnal leaves littering the woodland floor. "It is a nature lover's paradise here. I don't think there is any one time when Clumber is at its best.

"That is the wonderful thing about this property, it is magnificent all year round. Summer is nice if the sun is out and the trees are green, but then look at this wonderful autumn carpet we are coming through today - it is beautiful," he says with a big smile and an aura of serenity.

"Then you have a brisk cold morning in the winter as well, a quick walk around the lakeside is so stimulating. And, of course, in spring when everything is just popping through Clumber is splendid, it really is a magnificent place to visit."

Cycling is a popular pastime at Clumber Park

Cycling

With visitor numbers on the increase, and as many as 20,000 people visiting the historic park on baking hot summer days, it is clear that more than just Trevor firmly believe in the virtues of Clumber and all it has to offer.

And on days where the sun is soaring and sizzling the expansive open gardens and lake as well as the 20 miles of dedicated cycling trails often prove to be the biggest draws for the vast throngs of tourists.

The lush green gardens boast around 30 acres of pleasure grounds and are home to a large variety of ducks, swans and other birdlife.

Wildlife

The lake, with a circumference of four miles, was also used for boating as well as regular mock naval battles.

"This place is a haven for wildlife, it's thriving right now," I observe as I watch a majestic swan gently gliding along the still water. One of at least 60 swans enjoying the lake as we approach its edge. It's a great place to visit and forget any stresses.

"It's beautiful down here," agrees Trevor, "It's a whole new world down here and is fantastic. The autumn colours are beautiful," he adds as he looks back towards Clumber Chapel, with its magnificent 180ft spire climbing high into the sky.

A majestic swan

As the morning sun slowly begins to peak through the cloud cover, the park really begins to come to life as mothers with young childen begin to filter into the park and the quacking and chirping of the swans and other wildlife begins to grow and grow. It makes for a quite wonderful wildlife orchestra for any bird lovers taking a stroll around Clumber.

It makes for a quite wonderful **wildlife orchestra** for any bird lovers taking a stroll

We then move away from the lake to where Clumber House used to stand before it was destroyed by a fire in 1938 and demolished as a result.

"Clumber is like a huge country estate without its house," says Trevor with a gentle laugh. "Even now we get visitors turning up asking where the house has gone."

Clumber House was first destroyed in a fire in 1879, but the property was rebuilt by the defiant Duke.

When the 7th Duke died in 1928 the property passed on to his brother and then nephew, but the family couldn't afford to pay off the inheritance tax so in 1938 they decided to pull the mansion down bit by bit and sell off valuable posses-sions around the country to raise funds to pay the tax bill.

TIMELINE

1086
Clumber received its first mention in the Domesday Book.

1544
Henry VIII granted Roger and Robert Taverner lands in Clumber, which had belonged to Newstead Abbey, at 11 shillings per annum.

1707
In August John Holles, who was the 1st Duke of Newcastle, received a licence from the Crown to enclose 3,000 acres of his own land of inheritance at Clumber to make a park for Queen Anne.

1709
Clumber Park was enclosed as a deer park by John Holles.

Clumber chapel, with its magnificent **180ft spire** climbing high into the sky

A view from the bridge

I begin to reflect what the future has in store for this **splendidly British** of tourist attractions.

"Over the last few years we have made changes and new developments such as a restaurant refurbishment, the gift shop which is so vital in helping bring in extra revenue streams to re-invest back into Clumber, and £1.5m on our new visitor and interpretation centre to reveal the full history and wildlife at Clumber."

The future

As we come towards the end of my delightful day at Clumber, I begin to reflect what the future has in store for this splendidly British of tourist attractions.

On the face of it the future certainly seems to be more than bright, with the visionary National Trust reaching out into new and unique areas such as pop concerts and the opening of the Barkers fine dining restaurant to boost visitor numbers and revenue.

For Trevor, who is Clumber Park personified, the national delight also has a good future ahead.

Inside the chapel

The glass house

> "I guess more and more people are starting to discover places on their doorstep and the **simple pleasures** that it can bring."

"Over the last few years visitor numbers have steadily increased," Trevor says with evident pleasure. And who can blame him?

"I guess more and more people are starting to discover places on their doorstep and the simple pleasures that it can bring.

"The credit crunch means people are looking closer to home for places to visit. It is a team operation for all of North Nottinghamshire.

"We work with people from the wider tourist industry to boost the county's visitor numbers as well as our own," he adds as he again embarks on his passionate promotion of Nottinghamshire's vibrant tourist industry.

"It gives a massive boost to the local economy. There are competing parks and properties all over the country, but our objective is people living within 30 miles or so of Clumber. We know these people who visit us will keep coming back.

"I think it is kind of nice that whereas, once upon a time, Clumber was just a place where a family could enjoy themselves, it is now a place where thousands and thousands of families can come and enjoy themselves.

"There is mass appeal now, once it was exclusive . . . now it is inclusive."

The bridge

The gatehouse

"There is mass appeal now, once it was exclusive... now it is inclusive."

TIMELINE

1768
Work begins on Clumber House, after the 2nd Duke of Newcastle makes Clumber his family seat. The work is finally completed in 1778.

1879
A serious fire destroyed much of Clumber House in March.

1912
Another fire causes less damage, but the effects of the First World War and the Great Depression forced the abandonment of the mansion.

1938
The iconic Clumber House suffered a similar fate to many other houses during this period and was finally demolished.

TIMELINE

1939 - 1945
Clumber Park was used as an ammunition store with 60,000 tonnes kept in hundreds of stacks across the site.

1946
The National Trust bought the property for £75,000, £45,000 of which was raised by the public.

1955
The Army vacates Clumber Park, allowing the land to return to public use.

1980
The lake was partially rebuilt in the 1980s after suffering from the effects of coal mining in the area, which caused subsidence.

Interesting facts

- Clumber Park boasts Europe's longest double avenue of lime trees at three miles long, which lines the site's grand entrance.

- The man-made serpentine lake offers a four-mile walk around its banks and is home to more than 200 species.

- Clumber, which was first mentioned in the Domesday Book in 1086, was a monastic property in the Middle Ages.

- The estate is over 3,800 acres in extent, including woods, open heath and rolling farmland, while the serpentine lake covers 87 acres (352,000 square metres).

- The Clumber Park cricket pavilion was featured in an episode of the ITV cricket drama Outside Edge.

- Route 6 of the National Cycle Network passes through the park linking it to Sherwood Forest.

- 1,069 deer lived in Clumber Park in 1713, according to the findings of the park ranger.

- Clumber Park was used for secret trials of a 77-feet-long trench-digging tank code-named Nellie, which was capable of moving 100 tonnes of earth per minute.

- In November 1941, Winston Churchill travelled to Clumber Park under the alias Colonel Warden to inspect Nellie.

Facilities
- Toilets with baby changing facilities
- Buggies and child seats available for hire from cycle hire centre.
- Restaurant serving local, seasonal dishes
- Dogs welcome throughout the whole property
- Visitor Information Centre
- Discovery Centre
- Suitable for school groups & educational visits
- 183-pitch Caravan Club
- Available for functions

T 01909 544917   **E** clumberpark@nationaltrust.org.uk   **W** www.nationaltrust.org.uk

4 King's Mill Reservoir

King's Mill Reservoir

■ **EPISODE GUIDE:** Alan Cordin, countryside ranger at Ashfield District Council

SO HOW many of you motorists have driven into Mansfield along the A38, gone past the picturesque King's Mill Reservoir, and thought 'Oooh, how lovely?'

And how many of you have actually stopped at this hidden gem of the beauty spot world and sampled the wonderful wildlife and soothing surroundings on offer? . . . Come on, be honest now! The answer, sadly I fear, is not as many of us as it should be.

Hidden away just off the increasingly busy A38, the delightful lake is perhaps all too often overlooked as the daily pressures of work, never-ending chores and, well life in general, take their toll on our hectic schedules.

And when the rarity that is relaxation finally comes knocking on our door it is the more famous beauty attractions in North Nottinghamshire's impressive leisure portfolio such as Sherwood Forest, Sherwood Pines and Clumber Park that grab our attention.

But, just like its more illustrious neighbours, King's Mill Reservoir is a place packed with decades of unforgettable history, calming vistas, marvellous wildlife and is the perfect spot to ease away the stresses of life.

So, on a rather dull autumnal morning under a pale and lifeless looking sky, I set out to discover more with the help of countryside ranger Alan Cordin - a calm and knowledgable man responsible for managing the reservoir for Ashfield District Council.

A beautiful setting

And, as we made our way around the gentle 1.5 mile circumference, it became all too clear that this beautiful setting - which gained its royal title way back in the 12th Century when Henry II knighted local mill owner John Cockle after his wife had offered His Majesty food and shelter - is certainly a place worth getting to know.

"You're in a whole new world down here aren't you Alan?" I suggest, as the wind rushes through flapping tree branches.

"Yes it's a bit of a jewel in the crown of this area, because you are in countryside immediately from leaving the town," agrees Alan, no doubt made that little bit calmer thanks to the peaceful surroundings. "There's lots of nice relaxing water, there are water birds in their hundreds really.

The lake is home to Sutton Sailing Club

An idyllic place to be

"It's a lovely site. Not only is it **good for nature**, but it is also good for recreation."

But, despite the noisy roar of car engines at the southern end of King's Mill Reservoir, the site still retains a rather special feeling of being a haven for relaxation in the middle of nowhere.

There really is something rather magical about the sound of lapping water and the chorus of tweeting birds to bring on that warming sense of serenity and being at peace with oneself.

For wildlife lovers, as well as walkers, the delightful reservoir, which used to supply the surrounding corn grinding mills, is a place well worth exploring.

And as we continue our leisurely mid-morning amble I ask Alan to tell me a little bit about the type of work that goes into maintaining such an expansive body of water.

"What we have created here are some man-made reed beds to take out some of the nutrients and clean up the reservoir," says Alan, who clearly has a keen eye for detail when it comes to habitat management.

"It is a lovely site. Not only is it good for nature, but it is also good for recreation."

Alan's point is rather well timed, as we look to our left and spy the home of Sutton Sailing Club, which has called the reservoir its home since 1959.

"They regulary sail here and just behind us is the Mill Adventure base, where kids can come and have plenty of fun.

"I often come down here when I have some spare time," says Alan revealing his fondess for the reservoir he clearly takes great pride in looking after.

"It's a great place to have a walk around and just gets you away from everything. The only disappointment is the noise from the road, but there's no escaping the A38 and progress," Alan ventures with a hint regret.

"People want to get from A to B faster these days."

"The reservoir does have a lot of nutrients in it, which in itself is not harmful, but we are trying to reduce the level because we have a lot of weed growth. The reservoir is a lot cleaner than it used to be and we are getting the weed growth as a result."

My natural curiosity gets the better of me as I look out onto the lake at the rather large build up of green weed-looking plants calmy floating on the rippling water surface.

"So just how healthy actually is the reservoir?" I ask.

"It's green but it is perfectly harmless," Alan reassures.

"It is just normal blanket weed. Sometimes we do get a blue green algae appear, but with the reservoir getting cleaner we have not had that problem for quite a while.

"If we do get it, it is very rare and there is not much we can do about it really. It's just natural." he concludes philsophically.

"It's a difficult habitat to manage in some respects. It's a balancing act really because the sailing club require some things, wildlife requires other things, the fisherman need something else. It's a balancing act as I say, but generally it seems to work well."

That certainly seems to be the case, with the painstaking effects of wildlife habitat management at King's Mill having a positive effect as species thrive and bird numbers continue to grow, with Coots, Canada Geese and Mallards, in particular, enjoying renewed vigour.

Extensive knowledge

"There are some Mallards and Coots down there," Alan observes in the distance as his keen eye and extensive knowledge of the local bird population once again shines through.

"The Coot population has exploded over the last few years and this year are already on their fourth lot of young.

"There are more than 400 at the moment and that is down to good habitat, good breeding and plenty of food basically. We have also had four breeding pair of swans this year which is very healthy," Alan says, with what I detect is a touch of pride at his role in this welcome success story.

"As you can see, there is a pair of Canada Geese down there." He points to a spot just below our viewing platform.

"There are 20 more around so they are doing very well this year. They have had at least 15 young this year.

"We are on a migration route so we often get birds popping in to feed up on their way either coming from south to north or north to south. We're not far off the migration period right now actually, so we can expect one or two waders and things to pop in for food before they make their way south.

"Kingfishers are often seen here at the reservoir," he enthusiastically declares. "There is plenty of food for them and if you are a regular walker you will see them diving in for fish.

Coots certainly seem to be in their **ideal world** here, as we make our way round the lake

A bird paradise

"It's a bird lovers' paradise down here." Alan is clearly in his element as he then spots some swallows and swifts going about their day in the centre of the reservoir.

Our eyes then turn to a female Coot, the mother of many young, feeding her fluffy offspring some weeds with the loving care of a mother feeding a new-born baby. It is a beautiful scene to watch and, for me, and I suspect Alan too, wildlife and nature at its very best. Coots certainly seem to be in their ideal world here and, as we make our way around the lake, we're fortunate enough to see a superb contrast in age ranges from cute freshly hatched Coots right up to the mating pair responsible for such a healthy local population.

Perhaps the reason for the Coots' success is their protective nature. Alan eagerly explains: "Coots are quite aggressive. If you get any bird coming near the young, even a big swan, the Coot will fly at it and defend their territory and young."

I can't help casting my mind back to the summer's day when my partner Fiona and I were chased by a rather aggressive Australian swan when we attempted to picture it as we lazily cruised around Peasholm Park, Scarborough, in a pedalo. Ironically enough it was a swan pedalo now I think about it.

Maybe the swan got confused and simply wanted to mate with us, or maybe it just wanted a fight. But faced with this alarming threat we made our frantic getaway, at what must have been all of 1mph, with a certain amount of worry and legs cycling 19 to the dozen, as the black swan attempted to get into the boat and take a huge chunk out of Fiona's left leg.

The swan, which clearly had some sort of beef with us, then left us in peace and, to our great relief, we left the swan's world and returned to the safety of dry ground and a consoling ice cream. These Coots certainly are braver than I am.

TIMELINE

12th Century

King's Mill gains its name after King Henry II knighted Sir John Cockle, a mill owner, whose wife had offered him food and shelter.

1817

Portland Bridge, Britain's oldest railway viaduct, is constructed at the northern end of the reservoir for trains between Mansfield and Pinxton.

1837

The medieval pond at the King's Mill Reservoir site is expanded by the 4th Duke of Portland to help surrounding businesses survive.

1871

Portland Bridge falls into disuse following the building of another bridge further down river.

Looking for lunch

Historical delights

As we make our way to the northern corner of the reservoir, it is the historical delights rather than natural joys which now begin to come to the fore.

We come across Featherstone Close and King's Mill Road - to the untrained eye some nice looking family homes, but to the knowledgable Alan the former site of the old corn mill which gave King's Mill its modern-day name.

"Believe it or not the old mill used to be situated where these houses are now. It was a corn grinding mill. It went to ruin and unfortunately there was a big fire and most of it was destroyed," Alan reveals with a touch of sadness.

"The land was sold and we now have a small housing estate on it. It is a bit sad in some ways really," says Alan, who clearly has a great sense of loyalty and a bond with the reservoir. "It would be nice if the mill was still here, but things progess and move on."

A few paces later we cross onto a dam wall, a man-made structure of earth covered by concrete to make it look tidier and prevent it from being washed away. To our left a few seemingly insignificant bricks lay forlorngly on the soil - the last remaining evidence of the iconic former corn mill.

And, as if that wasn't enough history, Alan then turns my attention to Portland Bridge, which is the oldest surviving railway viaduct in England.

But, sitting a good 40ft or so away from the reservoir's edge, it is now disappointingly rather hidden away from general view as the surrounding trees and grass slowly begin to obscure its former grandeur. Had it not been for Alan, I would not have even known it was there.

The oldest viaduct

"It's quite a little treasure chest down here," I exclaim with a mixture of surprise, delight and admiration.

"It was completed in 1819," a thrust of excitement creeps into Alan's voice. "It was part of the old Mansfield to Pinxton line. A canal was built up to Pinxton and they were originally going to continue the canal into Mansfield.

"But because it was too steep, and they did not have a big enough water supply for all the locks needed they built what they called a tramway in those days," he continues.

"This was well before steam and the cart loads were pulled up to the summit at Kirkby-in-Ashfield by oxen.

"It is then a downhill run from Kirkby into Mansfield so they packed the oxen into empty wagons at the back and rolled them into Mansfield."

TIMELINE

1959
Sutton Sailing Club begins to use King's Mill Reservoir as a base.

1969
Mill Adventure base is built as a water activity facility for youngsters.

2003
King's Mill Reservoir is closed for two-and-a-half months after a breakout of toxic algae.

2005
A £1.4million transformation begins on the Mill Adventure Base.

Now we would simply use electricity-powered trains to shift great loads. Although it's clearly quicker and a sign of progress, I can't help but feel a tinge of disappointment at the loss of such ingenuity.

"That was to supply coal from the Derbyshire mines before Nottinghamshire really opened their mines," Alan adds. "The coal would then come along Derbyshire into the smelting works at Mansfield." Everywhere you look, it seems, there are still ever-lasting symbols and icons of the former coal industry so much embedded in the proud history of Nottinghamshire and Derbyshire and its hardworking people.

Unfortunately, as we are all too aware, Mansfield and Ashfield no longer has a coal industry to be proud of, but one thing the area can take great delight in is King's Mill Reservoir - a site as refreshing to visit as the cold water of the lake on a hot summer's day.

"It's nice here, it gets quite warm around the reservoir but there is a nice shade from the trees around the edge," says Alan, passionately promoting his beloved reservoir.

"You can hear birds singing and it's just so nice and peaceful.

"It's beautiful here for everyone. It's great to get back to nature, look at the birds, look at the butterflies.

"Welcome to King's Mill Reservoir everyone, come down here and enjoy it."

Interesting facts

■ King's Mill Reservoir acted as a head of water for a dozen mills along the River Maun, along with water meadows several miles away.

■ England's oldest railway viaduct stands at the northern end of the reservoir.

■ The area is a birdwatcher's paradise, with regular feathered visitors including the Tufted Duck, Great Crested Grebe, Grey Heron and Kingfisher.

■ King's Mill received its name from a mill on the north-east of the reservoir owned by John Cockle and his wife, who gave King Henry II lodging and breakfast.

■ The reservoir was developed by the 4th Duke of Portland to irrigate his land.

Facilities
■ Wildlife sanctuary
■ 1.5-mile circular walk
■ King's Mill Visitor Centre
■ Cafe, toilets and exhibitions
■ Sailing Club
■ Watersports

Contact: Sutton Sailing Club, 01623 559605 The Mill Adventure Base, 01623 556110

5 Hardwick Hall

Hardwick Hall

EPISODE GUIDE: Judy Williams

WHEN we study British history we learn about the key battles and wars that have shaped our nation's past, present and future, the often heroic Kings and Queens who led the country to glory and empire and the many great role models to have made their name.

But one person we sadly do not often hear about, at least if you live outside Derbyshire that is, is the inspirational Bess of Hardwick who left such an unforgettable mark upon this particular part of the country, which still lives on to this day through the county's tourist industry.

Bess, who was born Elizabeth of Hardwick in 1527 in the medieval manor house which once occupied the site of Hardwick Hall, rose from financial hardship to become the second richest lady in the realm behind Queen Elizabeth and enjoyed all the power and iconic status that came with such wealth.

Perfect role model

As well as being a very wealthy and important lady the determined Bess, who married her cousin, aged 13, in an effort to alleviate her family's financial difficulties, also provides the perfect role model to this very day.

With very little, Bess worked her way up to the top of British society, fighting her way upwards in the male-dominated world of the time, to become a self-made success story and create an ever-lasting legacy.

The visionary lady knew what she wanted and nothing, it seemed, could stop her march to the top.

'Bess' at Hardwick

The Entrance Hall

Nowadays her former Hardwick Hall home is one of Derbyshire's most important and popular tourist attractions, ensuring the legacy of this amazing woman lives on more than 400 years after Bess passed away at the unheard of age of 81.

And, with the tale of this fascinating woman in mind, I set out on a glorious summer's morning to meet my guide Judy

With very little, Bess worked her way up to **the top of British society**, fighting her way upwards in the male dominated world

Williams, who I soon found out had more than a bit of Bess in her, to learn all about the lady behind the tale and her richly-designed symbolic former home.

We begin our guide of the beautiful building in an impressive, if somewhat chilly, reception room, the place where all visitors to Bess's magnificent personal kingdom would have first entered.

"This area also doubled up as the servants' area so it would have been bustling with life with servants coming and going, with people eating and with the smell of food and chatter," says the bubbly Judy with real enthusiasm.

"When the important guests came in the servants would all stop what they were doing, stand to attention and keep their heads down while the guests sailed through into the main house."

This instantly strikes me as a rather odd notion. The thought of Lords and Ladies of the realm making their way through the common folk to get to the iconic Bess must have made quite interesting viewing. It is also a rather striking metaphor for Bess's own fairytale rise from local country girl to the very top of the British social ladder.

A splendid room

Taking one look around this splendid room, with its tall ceiling and strikingly expensive and rare decorations such as civil war weapons, a suit of armour as well as paintings and finely-crafted furniture, it is perhaps obvious why Bess was so eager to show it off.

"This is a very exciting room," Judy says animatedly revealing her fondness for all things Bess.

"Bess was not short of a penny or two and it shows in this room and the possessions she had. The children who visit this room love all the weaponry," she adds with a chuckle, before pointing to some chainmail of a 16th Century soldier on the wall. "This is a very rare item. We didn't realise just how rare it was but apparently it's very rare to get the leg-ins as well.

"The boys just love it. Some of the armour even has bullet dents in it when it was tested to see if the armour worked."

Judy is a retired lady who has a real air of drama and the theatrical about her.

And it's rather fitting that she does, as the talented Judy, when she's not being kind enough to be my personal guide, plays the role of Bess, dressing up in authentic costumes to enchant visitors when Hardwick Hall hosts special celebration events.

"This is my 15th season at Hardwick. I started the year before the Queen came to Hardwick on the anniversary of Bess moving in," the history-loving Judy reveals with pride.

"At first I was so scared. I felt I knew nothing, but I knew about Bess since childhood," she says rolling back the years fondly. "I read a book about her when I was a kid. I couldn't believe it when I visited Hardwick Hall for the first time.

"When I took early retirement I started here at Hardwick. I always liked history and used to teach drama, which goes very nicely with it," she adds with a slight chuckle.

"When I first started I was allowed to play Mistress Digby, Bess's favourite lady-in-waiting, giving the introduction talk.

"This year, once a month, I am going to be giving the introduction talk as Bess, so it is a bit of a promotion."

It certainly is a much-deserved promotion for Judy, whose refreshing passion and interest in her subject certainly helps to bring this particular period of history to life.

An imposing staircase

Judy then takes me up the most imposing set of stairs I have ever seen, as we wind our way steeply upwards towards the commanding High Great Chamber, one of Bess's private ceremonial rooms which were used for entertaining.

The steep gruelling climb reminds me of walking the famous 199 steps up to Whitby's Gothic abbey.

I'm also massively aware of just how daunting and nerve-wrecking this voyage into the unknown must have been for people visiting famous Bess for the first time.

Second only to Queen Elizabeth in financial terms, Bess was renowned across the land and was so close to the Queen she was even trusted to keep Mary Queen of Scots under house guard in the run up to her eventual execution.

You could say she had the allure and iconic stature of a modern day pop star or Premier League footballer.

"This staircase is just fantastic," Judy reveals in a respectful hushed tone. "In those days there would have been guards at every landing. This staircase was all about impressing guests and it certainly does just that."

Wealthy Bess, who at the time was the Countess of Shrewsbury following her latest and final marriage, ordered construction work on the magnificent Hardwick Hall to begin in 1590, to act as a symbol of her power and wealth and to send out an everlasting statement of her defiance as a woman come good in the male dominated world of the time.

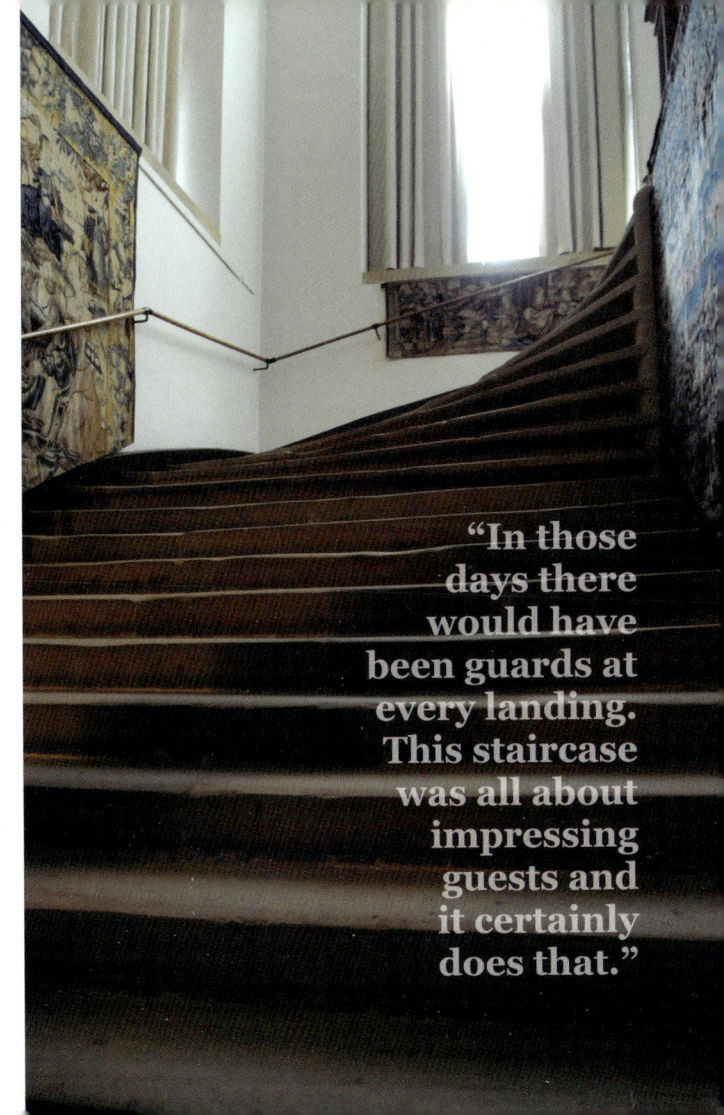

> "In those days there would have been guards at every landing. This staircase was all about impressing guests and it certainly does that."

A Royal reception

50

"People would walk up the stairs **breathless and overawed** and then, at the end of the room, there would be the lady of the house."

After nine years of painstaking work her personal castle was finally finished in 1599 and featured her initials E.S. taking pride of place at the top of each wing of the building and an unparalleled amount of glass, which was highly expensive at the time.

The result was an amazing building fit for any Queen in Europe and the most sumptious of all symbols of her wealth and popularity which fittingly had, just like Bess herself, a very large dose of glamour.

Once inside the High Great Chamber, I'm instantly filled with the 'wow' factor as the soaring ceilings and vast church-like glass windows allow waves of sunshine and light to flood in. It is a room that more than lives up to its glorious name.

"People would walk up the stairs breathless and over-awed and then, at the end of the room, there would be the lady of the house, Bess herself, waiting to receive her guests." explains Judy, who is a touch breathless herself.

"She would be sat there like a Queen. And for many people of this area who would not be able to go to London to see the real Queen, she was just like their Queen.

"She was terribly important," Judy continues with clear feelings of admiration for the lady she now occassionally pretends to be.

It seems many buildings of national historical importance around Britain are blessed with one impressive room or hall followed by another one through the next doorway.

And 16th Century Hardwick Hall, now owned by the National Trust organisation, is no different as Judy leads me on to the next "wow" room of this inviting national treasure - the fittingly named Long Gallery.

The Long Gallery, with its far wall stretching way into the distance, is the second widest, the biggest in volume in Britain and really is a true treasure.

It includes some of the most important paintings and tapestries in the nation, which have attracted the attention of emminent historians including Dr David Starkey looking to feature them in television documentaries.

The Long Gallery

Bess on a buying spree

"In 1591 Bess went up to London on a buying spree and bought 13 tapestries of The Story of Gideon from the Bible second hand for £321, 15shillings, 9p." Judy explains.

"I have the feeling that the ceilings in this room are this high because of the tapestries she bought."

It's not a typical woman's shopping spree but Bess certainly chose her purchases very wisely.

But, as you would expect, Hardwick guards such valuable relics very closely indeed.

"Dr David Starkey wanted to have our picture of Queen Elizabeth, but we said no. It's the only one we've got," Judy explains with an air of defiance which Bess would no doubt have approved of.

After our increasingly interesting tour of the top floor is completed Judy, who is really getting into the spirit of things

TIMELINE

1527
Elizabeth Hardwick, better known as Bess, is born in the medieval manor house, which once occupied the site of Hardwick Hall.

1540
Bess married her cousin, aged 13, in an effort to alleviate her family's financial difficulties.

1567
Bess marries the 6th Earl of Shrewsbury, in what was the last of her four marriages.

1584
Bess moves into the 'old' hall at Hardwick following a huge dispute with her husband, the Earl of Shrewsbury.

Old and new

like any good estate agent trying to sell a property, takes me down to the middle floor where Bess and her family spent most of their days.

It is also the area where the more recent owners of Hardwick lived and offers a stunning blend between the Elizabethan decor and more modern age items such as photographs.

"We're coming down the stairs to where Bess and her family lived," shouts Judy over the noisy thuds of our footsteps on the stone stairs. "This is a bit of a smaller area, the family lived off and on here right until 1960 so there is a good mixture of possessions here.

"We have bathrooms and toilets, a dressing room. It's a real transformation into the modern age. There are bedrooms at either end of the corridor with two social rooms in between, where the gatherings took place before people went off to bed."

Judy then takes our minds away from the present era and back to the fascinating world of Bess of Hardwick as she points out a spectacular piano in the centre of this spacious grandiose room, a perfect place for wining and dining England's greatest noblemen and women.

"This piano dates back to 1812. And there on the other side of the room is this peculiar oblong instrument which was played by young girls," says Judy.

"This room would have been full of life during Bess's time. There would be games, music and lots of room to chat with other people. It really was the nightclub of the Elizabethan era."

54

*"Bess had around **100 servants** who were tasked with making Hardwick Hall a delightful place to live in and visit and making sure the lady of the house and her **never-ending procession of important guests** were kept fed and watered."*

Bess had around 100 servants who were tasked with making Hardwick Hall a delightful place to live in and visit and making sure the lady of the house and her never-ending procession of important guests were kept fed and watered.

No doubt many of them living in the hustle and bustle of Hardwick would have looked upon Bess as an inspirational role model and dreamed of making their way up the social ladder towards fortune and a better life.

"It is a paradise here," Judy exclaims with a big beaming smile on her face. "I love it for the history, but it's good that the children who come here also love it. It is great for them to be able to see how people lived during that era, which is so very different to life nowadays.

Judy, now on a real roll, adds: "There was so much hierarchy. Hardwick Hall was the big business and the factory of the day.

"It is great finding out about the lesser known people who did the work around Hardwick.

"This house meant food on the table and a place to sleep for many people. Hardwick is a fantastic place for young and old to visit. There is something for everyone."

55

TIMELINE

1590
Construction begins on the 'new' Hardwick Hall.

1597
Bess of Hardwick moves in to her latest creation in October.

1599
The finishing touches are completed to the exhaustive Hardwick Hall construction.

1608
Bess dies aged 81.

1958
Hardwick Hall is handed over to HM Treasury in lieu of Estate Duty.

1959
The Treasury transfer the house to the National Trust in 1959.

Interesting facts

■ Bess of Hardwick became the second richest woman in the realm behind Her Majesty, with her marriage to Sir William Cavendish propelling her to fame and fortune.

■ For 15 years, Bess was responsible for guarding the doomed Mary Queen of Scots.

■ The initials 'ES' feature in the stone at the head of Hardwick Hall's six towers.

■ The imposing windows were a huge statement of Bess's vast riches and power, as glass was highly expensive at the time due to taxes.

■ An old rhyme captures the notable window features: 'Hardwick Hall - more glass than wall.'

■ The famous Long Gallery, which occupies the entire length of the east front, is the second longest of its kind in Britain.

■ The new Hardwick Hall is thought to have been designed by Robert Smythson.

■ Bess of Harwdick was also responsible for the building of Chatsworth House.

■ Much of Hardwick's present furniture and contents dates back to 1601.

Facilities
■ Restaurant
■ Souvenir shop
■ Drink and ice-cream kiosk.
■ Cycling permitted on parkland roads
■ Pay and display car parking
■ Babychanging and feeding facilities
■ Garden walks and beautiful lawns
■ Suitable for school parties
■ Accommodation - Two cottages ideally situated for exploring Derbyshire. www.nationaltrustcottages.co.uk

T 01246 850430   E hardwickhall@nationaltrust.org.uk   W www.nationaltrust.org.uk

6 Southwell Workhouse

Southwell Workhouse

EPISODE GUIDE: John Twelftree

IN THE modern-day compassionate Britain thousands of unemployed people across the nation flick through newspapers and head down to the Jobcentre on a daily basis in search of work.

They are safe in the knowledge that their homes and the welfare of themselves and their family will be taken care of thanks to Government money.

But nearly 200 years ago the unemployed folk of Nottinghamshire were not quite as lucky as the county became the pioneers of an all too different and harsher system aimed at getting the unemployed back into work.

The momentous, perhaps even notorious, social experiment - known as The Workhouse and introduced into the county at Southwell in 1824 at a cost of £6,500 - eventually evolved into the welfare system we see today.

A harsh way of life

This new system of poor relief offered the destitute shelter, food and, in the case of children, education in exchange for work. Sounds good I hear you think.

But rather than providing a haven for the poor and the answer to their dreams, the savage workhouse system, which was later expanded around Britain, offered a very harsh,

An austere home

punishing and, in some cases, I suspect, even soul-destroying way of life to discourage these unfortunate jobless from ever being out of work again.

So perhaps it was rather fitting then that when I arrived at Southwell Workhouse for my tour around this important national institution to meet my guide John Twelftree, a middle-aged man with grey hair and glasses along with a vast wealth of knowledge on this fascinating setting, I did so under a dark, dank and thoroughly miserable sky.

As we walk through the reception area the severe tone of the daunting building is immediately set by an impressive looking model in the centre of the room which, as John points out, demonstrates the fundamental principle behind the whole Workhouse system.

"In front of you, you see a model of the Workhouse, based on how it looked in 1824," explains John with the authority of any good museum curator. "The model shows what was the fundamental part of the Workhouse, and that is segregation.

"Family life ended when you came to the Workhouse and the building was constructed in such a way to ensure that. There were separate quarters for men, women and for children. These groups of people never met, they could only ever gaze at each other through the windows."

> "Family life **ended** when you came to the Workhouse and the building was constructed in such a way as to **ensure that**."

A female pauper is given a tedious task to pass the day

Two 'occupants'

"So it was a bit of a cheerless place then?" I ask John, perhaps rather stating the obvious.

"It destroyed family life," confirms John. "Perhaps the worst hit were the children who lost their parents. This was the absolute last resort. The other alternative during this period was perhaps dying under a hedge," he adds with a calm air of matter-of-factness. "There simply was nowhere else to go."

Southwell Workhouse, which was originally called Thurgarton Hundred Incorporated Workhouse before being renamed in 1836, was capable of housing 158 paupers from 49 parishes.

Perhaps one of the most enduring myths of the Workhouse - no doubt helped by the popular Oliver film - was that anyone unfortunate enough to find themselves confined into the soul-destroying system were stuck there for the rest of their days, with crime perhaps offering the only escape.

But, as John explains, this rather bleak and tear-jerking scenario was at its worst during the winter period when agricultural harvests in the surrounding countryside had been completed and jobs were scarce.

In the summer, though, it was an all too different affair, with the pioneering Workhouse housing just one inmate during one particular summer.

"There was plenty of work in the summer months," explains the history-loving John, whose passion for the era and Southwell Workhouse in particular begins to shine through. "After all, agriculture depended on horse and manpower - there wasn't

> "Perhaps the worst hit were the children who lost their parents. This was the **absolute last resort**...there was simply nowhere else to go."

anything else for farmers to use so there was a huge demand for labour.

"But come October, when the cattle was slaughtered, the ground ploughed and the harvest completed, there was little else for anyone to do. The farmers would dismiss them and they would come back to the Workhouse.

"The following February and March time they would all be gone again because of the huge demand for labour."

I find this quite a sobering thought I must admit, and one which certainly puts a whole new slant on the phrase 'boom and bust economy'.

A loss of liberty and loved ones

In today's Britain losing your job, devastating as it would be, would mean tightening your belt and perhaps giving up your football season-ticket or nights out on a weekend. In Victorian Britain it meant giving up your most cherished possessions - personal liberty and being with loved ones.

"The crucial thing was, did you have a job to go to?" John continues with enthusiasm rushing through his voice.

An isolating life

Knowing that you may never see your family again once the door closes behind you, it is rather easy to understand just why the workhouse was so hated

"If you had a job you could go. This wasn't a prison and people were not sent here by order of the court.

"You came here because you were destitute. But if you had a job and a means of support then you could go."

Hiring fairs were held around the area on a regular basis to showcase the many farming opportunities and trade jobs currently available - an event which must have given every single pauper a new-found sense of hope and determination to get their ailing life back on track.

"When they approached the Workhouse up Paupers' Path this would probably have been the largest building they had ever seen and it had a fearsome reputation," says John, who began working as a volunteer at Southwell Workhouse around 10 years ago. And, knowing that you may never see your family again once the door closes behind you, it is rather easy to understand just why the workhouse was so hated.

"They knew they were going to be separated," John emphasis with a deep powerful voice.

"They knew the diet was monotonous, they knew they couldn't just come and go as they pleased. In theory they could, but in practice it all depended on the master.

"Unemployment in the 19th Century was regarded as a crime,"says John, revealing just how much harsher Victorian society was back then." It was your fault you were unemployed. If you deserved to be punished for not having a job then you came here."

Worked to exhaustion

Once inside the highly-regimented system residents were worked to the brink of exhaustion, ordered to carry out the most mundane of tasks such as breaking pile after pile of rocks as an act of punishment for their perceived laziness and as a future deterrent. Women were ordered to carry out all the domestic duties around the Workhouse, which had to be entirely self-sufficient, including cooking, preparing vegetables, washing, cleaning and tidying.

Life certainly didn't get any easier for the men, who were put to work in an adjacent yard on a range of back-breaking tasks such as breaking wood, smashing rocks, dealing with coal and any other demeaning task the master saw fit to break the pauper's already shattered spirit.

"The master had to ensure that every single able-bodied person was kept working for every single minute of the day. And he did." reveals John. "A lot of their work carried out was utterly pointless and totally non-productive. It was just a case of keeping people busy and grinding them down."

And you thought your boss was a harsh taskmaster.

TIMELINE

1824
1824 - Southwell Workhouse is constructed by Reverend John Becher at a cost of £6,500.

1836
1836 - The Workhouse, originally called Thurgarton Hundred Incorporated Workhouse, is renamed Southwell Union Workhouse.

1913
1913 - Southwell Workhouse is renamed Greet House.

1920
1920 - During the 1920s a new hospital was established on the site for the care of terminally ill patients, and a mortuary was added.

A little light relief

As well as being forced to work the extremely long and gruelling hours, the paupers were also controlled through a strict disciplinary system with any act of defiance punished through a loss of rations, being sent to bed early and, in the most severe of cases, being flogged.

Clearly this was more than just a welfare state with a twist. It was an entire social experiment which, according to John, was created by a Government unsure of how to reduce the growing number of poor and the soaring expense.

And with poor relief costing a whopping £2m in 1784 and an even more staggering £6m by 1815 it is easy to see why they were desperate to ring the changes.

"The Government had become increasingly concerned with what to do," John explains with keenness. "The cost of the poor was rising enormously and this system was designed to control the poor and to control expense." I can't help but think controlling the expense is a phrase we hear all too often in the modern day of work. I guess some things just never change.

As we move inside the domineering building, which was purchased by The National Trust in 1997 following the threat that the building would be transformed into flats by developers, I notice that all the rooms look exactly the same.

Light-coloured brick walls, stone floors and a small fireplace sitting meekly in the centre of the room, all helping to create a rather bland and soul-less living experience.

Paupers were sent to bed early - in the winter it was around

Once sent to bed, they were **locked in their room** until the following morning

7pm - so the fires could be put out and money saved on the cost of coal and candles.

It was also no accident that the walls were painted a bright white colour, with the light shades reducing the need for candles. A cost-cutting measure I'm sure even Scrooge would have been proud to call his own.

Once sent to bed, they were locked in their room until the following morning. A sign of prison life creeping into the Workhouse if ever I saw one.

"It was a very regimented system," says John who, even though it is his job, still loves to devote his spare time to improving the Workhouse experience for visitors through research and doing whatever needs doing.

"Many of the masters had come out of the Army or Navy. They were used to controlling large amounts of people, to working 24 hours a day and, above all, they were used to enforcing strict discipline."

"It must have been quite a culture shock for the people before they got used to it," I suggest, my mind wandering back nearly 190 years to the arrival of the first inmates and the anxious desperate thoughts that must have been shooting nervously through their minds.

A view to the outside world

Many older people who had been married for 40 or 50 years were suddenly separated **and never saw each other again**

How would they cope with the loss of liberty and the harsh regime? How would they handle the loss of their loved ones, their very freedom and the back-breaking labour? Am I ever going to get out? No, I'd not have liked it or coped with my new surroundings too well either.

"People had to learn to tread very carefully and be aware of certain people," agrees John. "But the most awful thing about the Workhouse was the loss of family life, you lost your wife and children."

Many older people who had been married for 40 or 50 years were suddenly separated and sometimes never saw each other again. If that sobering thought doesn't spur you on to get a job then I guess nothing will.

But although it was a harsh and horrible existence, some small concessions were made to meet the strict religious needs of the Victorian period.

Paupers, who lived on a strictly-controlled and monotonous diet of bread and gruel for breakfast and supper and a dinner of potatoes, homegrown vegetables and five ounces of meat, were not allowed to work on Sundays.

Having worked something like a 72 hour working week it must have been a rest day they were extremely thankful to receive. But, for one day a year at least, things got even better for the helpless paupers, with what must have seemed a luxurious meal of roast beef, plum pludding, vegetables and tea and cake in the afternoon to celebrate Christmas Day.

Perhaps best of all though was the unheard of opportunity to be reunited with their cherished loved ones for the whole day. It must have been a joyous experience which reduced many, if not all, the inmates to tears.

"Families spent the whole day together," John explains with a big beaming smile."It must have been a really exciting and wonderful time for them."

Exciting and happy as that day may have been, Boxing Day must have been the biggest downer since the pauper was admitted for their first day at the daunting Workhouse.

It's now time to put John on the spot and I ask 'did the Workhouse system work?'

"Yes," he firmly replies without hesitation. "In rural areas it certainly worked. It relieved possible starvation.

"Once people came into the Workhouse they had food and they had accommodation, their children had education, they had free medical attention.

"For many it was a refuge." says John who is a passionate believer in the positive effect the Workhouse project had on shaping modern-day Britain.

"The Workhouse system was a significant social reform for the country. We can see the beginnings of the welfare state within the workhouse system."

The next time I'm sitting bored at work, I think I'll count myself rather lucky. At least I will be heading home at the end of the day to be with my loved ones.

OUR GUIDE

John Twelftree joined the Workhouse shortly before it opened and performs a variety of tasks including room stewarding and working in the education department

"I enjoy coming here, it reveals a part of our history that, if we didn't do something about it, would disappear.

"The poor are not popular, battles, kings and queens are what we learn about, but this affected a vast section of the population for hundreds of years."

TIMELINE

1929
The New Poor Law system was disbanded and workhouses or institutions were handed over to local authorities.

1948
The building gradually evolved following the introduction of the modern welfare system and provided temporary homeless accommodation until 1976.

1997
The Workhouse's future is secured after being purchased by the National Trust.

Interesting facts

- Southwell Workhouse could hold 158 paupers and catered for paupers from 49 parishes across the area.
  The building is the least altered workhouse structure in existence today and almost unchanged since the 19th century.

- Southwell Workhouse was originally called Thurgarton Hundred Incorporated Workhouse.

- The Workhouse once had just one inmate as summer agricultural employment reduced demand.

- Those who entered the workhouse were called 'inmates' and, in accordance with the instructions of the Poor Law Commission, the inmates' own clothes were taken away from them and each was given a uniform to wear.

- Southwell Workhouse was one of the first workhouses in the country.
  Around 600 union workhouses were established throughout the country by 1840 using Southwell as their blueprint.

- Male inmates were housed in the east wing of the Workhouse, while women were housed in the west wing.

Facilities
- Free parking
- Gift shop selling specialist publications as well as fresh, seasonal garden produce
- Suitable for school groups
- Babychanging facilities.
- Regular family events

T 01636 817260   **W** www.nationaltrust.org.uk/theworkhouse@nationaltrust.org.uk

7 Chatsworth

Chatsworth House

EPISODE GUIDES: Kay Rotchford and Sue Brown

THOSE FILM buffs amongst you may instantly recognise the picturesque Chatsworth House from cinema and television adaptations of some of Britian's most popular period novels.

The charming and captivating Peak District delight has played home to a host of film crews, including the 2005 film version of Jane Austen's Pride and Prejudice, and most recently The Duchess, which tells the fascinating life story of Georgiana Cavendish, the 5th Duchess of Devonshire, and stars the equally beautiful Kiera Knightley.

Nestled away in the Peak District, Chatsworth House offers a fantastic blend of beautiful secluded scenery, stunning architecture and 16th Century authenticity making it the perfect place to film the latest blockbuster.

But, as I found out, when I was lucky enough to be given a personal tour around the eye-catching estate, there is much more to it than just a good film location.

Within seconds of my entrance into the north hall the sheer splendour and magnificence of Chatsworth is visible for all to see with the Italian marble floor setting the perfect tone for the rest of the tour.

Impressive features

The impressive floor, which was put in by the 6th Duke of Devonshire in the 19th Century, has surprisingly only recently been discovered by the estate owners after being hidden away for many years by a carpet.

"It was protected by a carpet, but it seemed a real shame to hide something as beautiful as this way," explains one half of my guide team, Sue Brown. "We have been assured by the conservators that the floor will not be damaged without the carpet on it."

At the far end of the spacious corridor lays an even more

Within seconds of my entrance into the north hall the sheer **splendour and magnificence** of Chatsworth is visible for all to see

spectacular staircase, which seems to convey all the grandeur and power of the estate in a similar way that the famous opulent staircase did on the doomed Titanic.

Above and around the staircase proudly hangs a variety of beautiful paintings, dating as far back as 1692, depicting the life and times of Roman emporer Julius Caeser as well as around 10 2nd Century Roman busts.

"The pictures have been conserved and restored in rather dramatic fashion," says Sue, who as a guide is as good as you get. "The ceiling was seen to be sagging in 1936 so there was little time to waste with the restoration project. It took two years to complete."

Amongst the pictures on show are Caeser declaring himself Emperor, his momentous crossing of the English Channel and his brutal assassination.

And, as Sue reveals with evident pleasure, it is thanks to the history-loving 6th Duke of Devonshire that Chatsworth is the proud home of such treasures.

"A lot of the ancient pieces that we have were bought by the 6th Duke," she adds. "It was a big personal fascination of his, he just loved to collect and he certainly chose wisely."

> We then move on to **The Film Exhibition** area, which proudly showcases Chatsworth's many appearances upon the big screen

And not surprisingly the room has proved to be a massive hit with youngsters and, as we enter the snug little room, we're greeted by two playful children aged around seven or eight years-old, trying on the wigs on offer.

"We have had a lot of films made here at Chatsworth," says Kay, as she is watched over by a life-size model of Hollywood star Kiera Knightly. "This is a really interesting place because it has got history, glamorous costumes from The Duchess film and some excellent artefacts.

"The Family Discovery Room is new to Chatsworth but it is an excellent addition. It was supposed to be just for the kids but the adults love to try the clothes on," she adds unable to contain a boisterous laugh at the thought.

"The Duchess was a very good film," Kay continues, raising her voice to compete with the noisy group of schoolchildren who have just entered the exhibition.

"It was very representative of the story. It was quite exciting when the crews were here and the visitors really enjoyed it.

"It gives everyone a buzz."

This comprehensive and impressive collection certainly helps to add to the ever-growing appeal of Chatsworth and provides art lovers with a splendid journey through the centuries of the genre.

We then move on to The Film Exhibition area, which proudly showcases Chatsworth's many appearances upon the big screen through a series of interactive displays and props from the film which is already appealing to both young and old.

Visitors are even given the chance to try on authentic period clothes in the Family Discovery Room.

The Cascades

> "**Chatsworth has so much to see and do**, it takes more than just one visit to soak up what we have got on offer."

"I'm a bit disappointed by it all," Sue interjects with a merry, if but a touch rueful chuckle. "I missed the crews being here and missed out on all the fun."

But for anyone who did miss the big day, the Film Exhibition certainly does a very good job at conveying exactly what went on.

Following the release of The Duchess, Chatsworth, which boasts 105 acres of stunning colourful gardens and one of the nation's best water cascade features, saw a clear rise in visitor numbers with people from far and wide eager to see for real the place they had enjoyed so much on the big screen.

After our brief flirtation with the present day we move seamlessly back down the centuries and into The Great Chamber, which is one of a series of rooms which come together to form the luxurious State Apartment suite.

The delightful suite was developed by the first Duke of Devonshire in a bid to attract King William III and Queen Mary to Chatsworth House. But, despite the large amount of money lavished on the rooms, it was all in vain and the Royal couple never made their visit.

A rich history

The theme of learning again comes to the fore as we progress into the Building History exhibition, which takes visitors on a fascinating trip through the years to celebrate everything that is good and famous about this most delightful of stately homes.

For Kay, who I sense has more than just a work-related passion for the 12,310 acre Chatsworth site, being able to educate, enthuse and entertain visitors in this way is a key element to Chatsworth's ongoing success.

"Each year we always try to keep it fresh and offer something different," she explains.

"We get visitors that come back every year and it is good to be able to give them something different. Chatsworth has so much to see and do, it takes more than just one visit to soak up what we have got on offer."

Nowadays the 126 room estate, of which nearly 100 are closed to visitors, rocks with the contented chatter of happy families enjoying their day out.

But back in the time of the 6th Duke, Chatsworth moved to the music of the era, with big social gatherings taking place on a regular basis in the grand State Music Room, which we are now passing through.

As we saunter through, the gentle hum of classical music fills the background with enchanting sounds and a classical 17th Century Harpsicord sits waiting to be played in a corner. It must have been a delightful place to mingle hundreds of years ago when the room buzzed with people and activity.

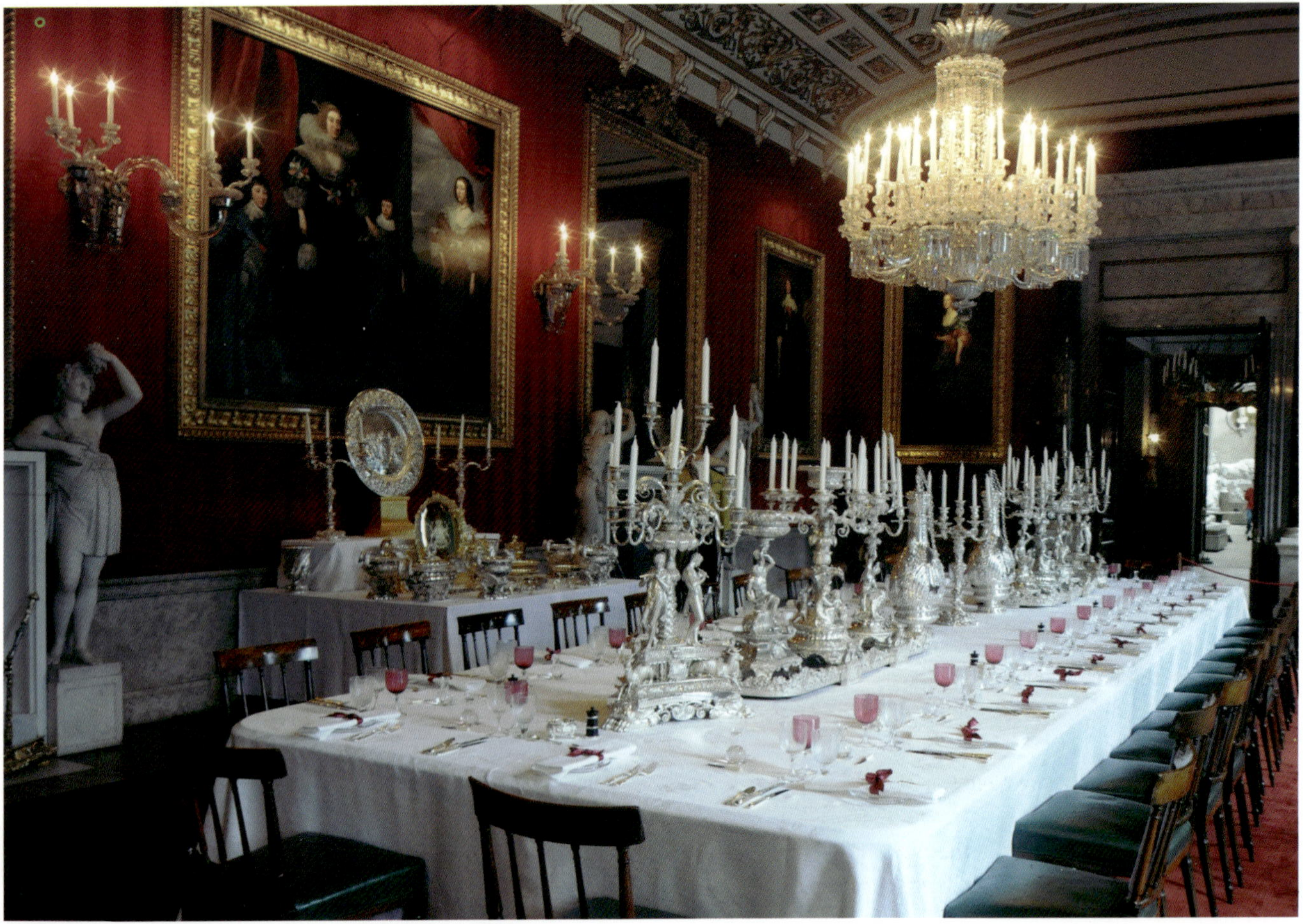

Everywhere we turn it seems there are more and more spectacular and lavish paintings, busts, artwork and decor

Sue and Kay then guide me into a brightly lit gallery area and to an appealing painting which reveals an often unknown secret in Chatsworth's long and distinguished history.

"During the war Chatsworth was turned into a school for girls who were evacuated here," Kay reveals in the full flow of a good art historian. "This picture was painted showing the girls using one of the state rooms as a dormitory.

"It must have been quite daunting for them at the time, but they just got used to the place after a while, it was just where they lived."

Following our departure from the gallery, Chatsworth appears to resemble something more like a building site. But fear not, the attraction is not crumbling down. We have just entered an area currently undergoing a huge five-year restoration plan to preserve the beauty of the historically-rich Chatsworth and create additional space to showcase many more of the house's array of treasures.

From what I have already seen it is rather hard to imagine that Chatsworth has any more treasures to reveal.

Everywhere we turn it seems there are more and more spectacular and lavish paintings, busts, artwork and decor.

And, right on cue, we glide into a long thin corridor stretching far into the distance and littered with a beautiful range of ancient and contemporary art and the Sculpture Gallery which would not be out of place at any London art gallery.

"The two corridors have an excellent range of old and new. Here we have Egyptian memorial tablets set into the wall. The oldest is nearly 4,000 years old.

"Then we have the modern art of Lucian Freud and Sean Scully in contrast," Sue adds expertly.

Last but not least is the captivating and historically significant 19th Century north wing, which was added thanks to the relentless improvement work of the 6th Duke and finally completed in 1832 - just in time for the visit of a young Princess Victoria.

The Sculpture Gallery

It was in this magical room that the young Royal enjoyed her first grown-up meal. As my mind wanders back to nearly 190 years ago, I cannot help feel a tingle of excitement and delight to be in this awe-inspiring room where such a key moment in the nation's history took place.

Awe-inspiring is perhaps the perfect way to describe this most wonderful of settings. And whether you want to enjoy the beautiful sunshine in the lush green and expansive gardens or amble through the amazing collection of artwork amassed by the Devonshire family, it is clear that this superb jewel in the Derbyshire tourist armour has something for everyone, whether young or old, local or foreign, poor or rich.

"Chatsworth is a warm and friendly place," says Kay with a great sense of belief in the whole Chatsworth package.

"We don't have 'Keep off the Grass' signs, we let people take pictures and we have lots of things to keep people entertained. It is very relaxed here and I think that is key. We have a warm lived in feeling and we pride ourselves in the friendly nature of our staff.

"It is a fantastic day out for everyone. There is modern, traditional and contemporary art, a wonderful history, a huge garden, water features. What more could anyone want?

Well she would say that I hear you say.

She certainly would . . . but it is also very true.

"A wonderful history, a huge garden, water features. What more could anyone want?"

Facilities
- Farmyard
- Woodland adventure playground
- Chatsworth Garden Centre
- 1,000 acre park
- Farm shop
- Restaurant
- Picnicking facilities
- The Chatsworth Fishery
- 105 acre gardens with famous cascade waterfall

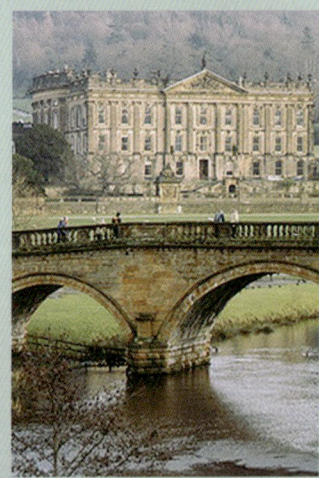

T 01246 565300 **W** www.chatsworth.org